Forward

Books about what our response should be toward children are often written with the theme of what our responsibilities are toward children. In this devotional material Ray Hawkins points out more than this. He sheds light on the remarkable lessons we are privileged to learn from children, who God has appointed to express the heart of heaven. The author points out that we may never have known of God's priority care and concern for children if not for the Jesus stories and teachings in the Word of God.

Many of us have heard the words of Jesus which refer to us imitating children's trust and humility which sometimes sounds like a 'nice' thing to do, however some of us have not fully grasped the meaning of these words. The author throws new focus on these fundamental truths and the serious consequences of not following the example of children.

The millstone necklace devotion reflects the author's intimate knowledge of the qualities of a child and how Jesus elevates the child to be on His level. These words should challenge our attitudes and actions toward children and how we welcome them, their ideas, which is synonymous with how we welcome God. Our sometimes questionable values can lead children astray in our consumer driven society which angers God when we become an obstacle between Him and children. The author further confronts us about how we prioritize children, particularly in a society which is becoming increasingly self satisfying – where children are sometimes seen as a commodity, lacking status. The warnings here about a milestone should be frightening to the reader.

It is a privilege to join with children in celebrating their uniqueness, to embrace childhood as an important stage in the formation of the whole person. Family, friends, church and the local community are responsible for creating an environment that promotes children's well-being. Respecting the image of God in every child demands a Christ-like response to nurture them throughout childhood. The author confronts us about a number of issues such as what kind of inheritance we plan for our children- is it unfading and incorruptible? How do we handle the disappointments and frustrations which are part of caring for children? Do we corrupt the ideals of youth with our cynicism? Do we exasperate the children in our care? How do we prioritize children in our care? What stories of God's grace, goodness and glory am I sharing with children and adults? What intellectual, moral and spiritual treasure do I invest into the hearts and minds of my children or those in my care?

Have I taught them their worth to me and therefore to their Heavenly Father? Am I providing a stable loving home for my children?

It is a privilege to be part of a child's life. Children are a promise of hope for every generation. Let us take up the author's challenge and learn from and engage with children in ways which honour them.

Mrs Jacqui Purnell, Early Childhood Care and Development Technical Advisor.

Married to David, World Vision East Asia Regional Office - Senior Director Operations.

Mother of three children.

About Ray Hawkins

A Rockdale boy (NSW) who was an early Christmas present to his parents being born 18th.12.1938. He grew up in a working class home, worked as a lathe operator for a car engine repair firm then a labourer with his father's light steel fabrication business. He was sent to Sunday school at the local Church of Christ where he made his confession of faith and was baptized. At 21 years he was accepted as a student at the Churches of Christ Woolwich Bible College (Sydney). In 1963 Ray became the Student President of the College. That year he met his wife to be, Mary, who came to College for a two year missionary course. In 1964 they were married and over the years they became parents of three children.

Their major ministry emphasis has been in establishing 2 new Churches in N.S.W. and preventing one from closure in Qld. They also ministered in England. Ray has been N.S.W. Conference President on two occasions, and N.S.W. President for the Ministers' Association. He has been a Chaplain to the Green Hills Retirement village and Nursing Home (N.S.W.). For 18 years he was involved with the Tenambit/Morpeth Rotary club becoming President and later made a 'Paul Harris Fellow'. Ray also became active with the 'Walk to Emmaus' movement and became Community Spiritual Director for Tasmania.

In his later years and with Mary went three times as part of short term mission trips to Africa. Out of that experience he wrote the 31 day devotional 'The Neurotic Rooster.' (It was a finance raiser for Eagles Wings in Zambia.) Now retired to Beauty Point, Tasmania with Mary who is a multi-published Inspirational Romance writer he still preaches and is involved in establishing a Christian Fellowship there.

He is a regular contributor to 'The Upper Room' devotional magazine as well as having numerous articles, poems and Studies from Scripture printed throughout his ministry.

Children: God's Special Interest
Published by Even Before Publishing;
a division of Wombat Books
P. O. Box 1519, Capalaba Qld 4157
www.evenbeforepublishing.com
www.wombatbooks.com.au

© Ray Hawkins 2011
Design and layout by Even Before Publishing
Child painting photo: istockphoto
Feet photo by Sarah Rowan Dahl

ISBN: 978-1-921633-35-5

National Library of Australia Cataloguing-in-Publication entry
Author: Hawkins, Ray
Title: Children: God's special interest/ Ray Hawkins
ISBN: 9781921633355 (pbk.)
Subjects: Children.
             Meditations.
Dewey Number: 242

All rights reserved. No part of this publication may be reproduced, stored in, or introduced into a retreival system, or transmitted, in any form, or by any means (electronic, mechanical, photocopying, recording or otherwise) without the prior written permission of the publisher.

Contents

Heaven's Promise to the Fatherless	7
The Touch That Blesses	9
Heaven's Estimation	11
Beware the Millstone Necklace	13
Be On the Lookout	15
Children of the Childless	18
From the Lips of Children	20
The Heart's Key	22
Crowns, Bestowed by Grandchildren	24
Preparing the Child for Life	26
Consequences	28
A Poor Boy's Gift	30
Molech	32
Against the Odds	35
The 'O' Word	38
Some Children Do Have Them	40
A Parent's Joy	42
Hidden Treasure	44
The Garment of Love	47
A Child's An Indicator of a Father's Suitability	50
Beware the Phantoms of Life	52
A Child's Faith in Old Age	54
When a Child Dreams	56
Fathers with Foresight	59
The Shepherd's Rod	62
The Beauty of the Unseen Child	64
The Promised Child	67
The Child Who Came	69
The Child of Nazareth	72
When it will be Safe to Play	74
Becoming Children of God	76
I See A Child	79

Introduction

The following devotionals aim to give insights from Scripture about God's heart for Children. He has entrusted the care of these precious lives into the arms and hearts of parents, and to a lesser extent, to governments and communities.

There does seem to be a Scriptural principle about the moral and spiritual health of families and communities based upon the way children and the vulnerable are treated. From all indications, we live in a sick society.

Our Lord doesn't expect us to live with a ghetto mentality and so withdraw from confronting the World's sickness with His healing grace. We are to offer His remedies and display His wisdom and power by his Holy Spirit operating in our own life, our family, and our priorities. This has special significance for Christian parents. Our Heavenly Father desires us to honour Him by honouring each other and especially our children. God has not left us in ignorance as to how we can do this as He has recorded His intentions in the Scriptures. That places a responsibility on our shoulders to open it, read it, search out the issues and then apply the principles.

There are numerous instructions and examples within God's word by which we are to learn and live. I would like to share with you some of those dealing with children whether your own, the orphans, or the neglected. I also wish to share with you the wonderful promises of God relating to the Promised Child.

At the end of each devotional is a 'reflection/action' sentence designed for you to record anything that stirs within your heart as you read what was set for the day!

Raymond N. Hawkins

Day 1

Heaven's Promise to the Fatherless

Reading: Psalm 94

Key verse: *Our Father in heaven, hallowed be your Name, your kingdom come, your will be done on earth as it is in heaven.*

Matthew 6:9,10

Karma will not motivate; Emotionalism will not persevere; Atheism will not see any purpose in showing compassion for the weak, vulnerable and the fatherless. Compassion in the soul is birthed by Faith and Conscience.

From the Christian perspective, rising up on behalf of the fatherless is a 'Family' matter. The scriptures tell us that our Heavenly Father has a special interest in the weak, the widow, the orphaned and the refugee. 'A father to the fatherless, a defender of widows, is God in his holy dwelling.' (Ps.68:5).

James, a servant of God and the Lord Jesus Christ wrote, 'Religion that God our Father accepts as pure and faultless is this; to look after orphans and widows in their distress and to keep oneself from being polluted by the world.' (James 1:27).

How do we know that the Eternal and Holy God is interested in the fatherless? From a look around the crisis scenes of the globe where such children cry from neglect and abuse, it is hard to see the footprints of God. We may never have known of His priority care concerns for such children without His written Word, and the life of His only begotten Son, Jesus. In them God has made His will known. He has placed upon the shoulders of His people the burden and privilege of representing Him to the widows, orphans, weak, and displaced. We are His 'fingerprints,

His footprints, His fragrance.'

'He (the Father) defends the cause of the fatherless and the widow, and loves the alien, giving him food and clothing. And you are to love those who are aliens...' (Deut. 10:18, 19).

When we seek to stand up for the cause of the exploited or neglected children of any society we will face opposition from godless vested interests. They are only interested in what they can make out of a child. When a child's economic value is finished, they throw him or her on the 'scrap heap'. Such wickedness makes a person imagine God is blind to their deeds and deaf to the cries of the afflicted. The Scriptures declare very forcibly that God has His accounting Day where justice will be executed.

There is a cost involved in helping the oppressed. There is also a promised blessing. 'At the end of every three years, bring all the tithes of that year's produce and store it in your towns, so that the Levities (who have no allotment or inheritance of their own) and the aliens, the fatherless, and the widows who live in your towns may come and eat and be satisfied, and so that the Lord your God may bless you in all the work of your hands.' (Deut. 14:28, 29). In Deut. 26:13 this contribution to the welfare of the needy is called, 'the sacred portion'. God has given His people the privilege of being involved in a ministry that expresses the heart of Heaven.

Prayer: Eternal God, what an awesome privilege we have to call you 'our Father'. You, the Creator, have become our Redeemer through Jesus Christ, and have made us part of your eternal family. May your heart of compassion for the fatherless and the widow beat strong in us so that we too may reach out to care and protect them! This is our desire in Jesus Name.

Reflection/Action: Lord, what can I offer to the fatherless children as an expression of your 'sacred portion?'

Day 2

The Touch That Blesses

Reading: Mark 10: 13-16.

Key verse: *He took the children in His arms, put His hands on them and blessed them.* Mark 10: 16

His face was set. His stride purposeful! He was on His way to Jerusalem, knowing full well the cross would be His last embrace. Jesus, however, never lost sight of the Father's wider ministry to others. At an unknown disciple's house in an unnamed village the Lord of Glory, Jesus, reveals God's heart for children.

Did Jesus pause a while to enjoy a rest and hospitality at the place, or maybe stay the night? Word of course spreads so quickly in a village when a stranger appears, or a person of repute, such as a Rabbi, arrives. In Mark 10:13-16 implies that Jesus was well known personally or by reputation. No parent or guardian would consider taking a child to be blessed by someone not known or respected.

The stream of people was constant. They persisted in meeting Jesus so that He would simply touch their child or children. This persistence overwhelmed the zealous concern of Jesus' Disciples, the 'famous 12' and one can only guess their irritability. The word for their rebuke of the children and parents has the sense of being unjust and rude.

The records of Jesus ministry tell us that He was never distressed by the needs of those who sought Him out. It was the hypocrite and the conceited that annoyed Him. Here we also see that being an obstacle between children and Himself, regardless of motive, warrants His displeasure.

The feeling behind 'indignant' in the NIV has the idea of Jesus being in pain at the treatment of the children. It is a strong word speaking of deep emotion. In my mind there is no doubt such emotion continues in Heaven due to the way the children of the World continue to be treated.

The hands of a carpenter turned Rabbi would have been strong, probably showing a callous or two. These hands had touched a leper and made him whole. They had caressed the eyes of the blind, restoring sight. These hands had lifted the fallen and raised the dead. Now they not only touched the children, they embraced them.

I wonder what became of these children? Can you imagine their parents or guardians reliving the incident for them across the years? To have hands placed upon one's head was a setting apart, a blessing bestowed, an identification. When Jesus does that, whether physically as here, or into your life by His Spirit through faith in Him, life and the future are never the same. When we relax in Jesus, take Him at His Word as a child, we discover the impact of the kingdom of God into our lives.

Following on from this story is an encounter which highlights what Jesus referred to about becoming like a little child. A rich young ruler came seeking confirmation of eternal life. He didn't allow Jesus to touch him, lay hands on him, ordain him. Why? His wealth, pride and status prevented him accepting the child-like spirit. He missed out. He went away, sad. No one ever rejects Jesus and His blessing, and walks away from Him joyfully.

Prayer: I remember the time when you touched my life by your word and Spirit precious Lord. You changed my life and destiny. As I move through life may somehow or other you touch others, especially children, through what I say, how I live, and by my prayers. This I ask for your glory. Amen.

Reflection/ Action: What practical way will I be able to encourage a child today?

Day 3

Heaven's Estimation

Reading: Matthew 18:1-14

Key verse: *I tell you the truth, unless you change and become like little children, you will never enter the kingdom of heaven.*
Matthew 18:3

On His way to Jerusalem, Jesus paused awhile in Capernaum. This was a place in which He had exercised a wide ministry. Near here he had called fishermen and a taxation official to be disciples. It was a city in which Jesus did some mighty works, and gave a very controversial sermon about His body (John 6).

Little did the populace know it was the final ministry tour of their celebrity. Did the place where Jesus stayed belong to Peter's mother-in-law (Mark 1:29-31)? It's evident from the account in Matthew 18:1-4 the child Jesus placed before His disciples was not amongst strangers. What Jesus said, using this child (belonging to a family member or friend), must have been doubly embarrassing. '(Jesus) called a little child and had him stand among them. And He said; "I tell you the truth, unless you change and become like little children, you will never enter the kingdom of heaven. Therefore, whoever humbles himself like this child is the greatest in the kingdom of heaven".'

Along the way to Capernaum the disciples had been heatedly debating who was the greatest. How strange is the human heart and mind! The Lord had told them He was heading towards His death and His closest friends just didn't get it. They spin fantasies of their own importance instead of helping Jesus prepare for His appointment with the cross. The Master bided His time. He waited for the opportune moment to pierce the conscience, awaken the spirit, and evaporate their fantasies.

To take a child, probably known to most disciples, and use him as a visual teaching aid, would have been rather unsettling. Imagine, that boy goes home and tells his story. Before long it spreads, and is without doubt embellished. Jesus wasn't vindictive in doing this. He saw beyond the cross to their future ministry. The Master's message here was painful though therapeutic. For the disciples and for all disciples of Christ ever since, there were and are, more 'therapeutic' lessons to learn.

Greatness, in God's view, is a universe away from Society's estimation. Celebrities are feted, followed, idolised. Something within all of us envies such people. Celebrities in God's view are those who have the heart of a child, the repentance of a convert to grace and the obedience of faith. These are more often than not, unknown or ignored by the World. Very few of us find it easy to have the mind set of a child. It goes against the grain of the soul.

The value system of Heaven is upside down from the World's priorities. This is re-enforced by Jesus, 'The greatest among you will be your servant. You know that the rulers of the Gentiles lord it over them, and their high officials exercise authority over them. Not so with you. Instead, whoever wants to become great among you must be your servant, and whoever wants to be first must be your slave – just as the Son of Man did not come to be served, but to serve, and to give His life as a ransom for many.' (Matthew 20:25-28).

Prayer: Grant to me Heavenly Father a genuine desire to understand what it means to 'welcome a little child' in the name of Jesus. May I in understanding do it! Amen.

Reflection/ Action: Lord, do I have the 'sceptre' or the 'towel' attitude in my heart concerning how I approach the Christian life?

Day 4

Beware the Millstone Necklace

Reading: Luke 17:1-3
Key verse: *Whoever welcomes a little child…in my name welcomes me.* Matthew 18:5

I wonder how clean the little child was that Jesus used as His visual aid to teach some eternal Truth? Had he been playing in the dusty street? How well were his sanitary arrangements? Was he in need of a change or a wash? Little children need protection, supervision, feeding, changing. They can be nuisances, sleep disturbers, cheeky without malice and yes, naughty. Yet, with one look of their eyes that shine with affection for you can make all the disturbances, discipline and other costs of no importance.

My mind pictures a shy, self-conscious, grimy-faced child looking at Jesus through lowered eyes. With hand on the child's head, Jesus elevates the worth all of children. For Christians, it's an identification issue. Jesus talks about the opportunities adults have for welcoming a child. In so doing, a special partnership is unconsciously embraced. The adult has also welcomed Jesus.

The Gospels portray Jesus as identifying Himself with the non-powerful of society. Matthew 25 is the classic example where Jesus is seen in the guise of the hungry, the thirsty, the stranger, the sick, and the prisoner. In teaching these things Jesus makes a statement about the inherent worth of a person in God's eyes. As with the Matthew 25 passage so with the child, how we treat such people are pointers to our relationship with Jesus.

We live in a society that treats these words of Jesus with contempt. Even Christendom has become immune to the plight of those Jesus highlighted. Children especially are exploited, abused, ignored, eliminated, as though they were unwanted toys, unprofitable machinery and without rights as a 'yet to be born!' The Church of Christ must be their advocate. The Church must also warn of God's wrath stored up for those who remain unrepentant about such treatment.

The word in the NIV written as 'sin' comes from the Greek 'skandalon' meaning a trap laced with bait. It also has the idea of being a stumbling block deliberately set to cause a fall. Men and women deliberately enticing or coercing children into immorality, unbelief, enslavement will face the full force of Heaven's justice. Jesus said if a person is tempted to do such an abominable thing, go for a swim in the lake with the big millstone as a necklace. He also shows, using graphic imagery, it is better to remove from your life whatever causes a 'skandalon.' The outworking of not doing so has eternal, unpleasant, consequences. In Matt.5:29, 30 Jesus said, in what is metaphorical language, that it is better to cut off from your body the offending part than to have your whole body cast into Gehenna. God has given us a most precious privilege. To deliberately choose to receive a child, regardless of their appearance or status, and to honour them, is tantamount to welcoming Jesus. "Whoever welcomes a little child like this in my Name welcomes me. But if anyone causes one of these little ones who believe in me to sin, it would be better for him to have a large millstone hung around his neck and to be drowned in the depths of the sea." (Matthew 18:5,6).

Prayer: I seek your forgiveness Lord Jesus for the times I have been a 'stumbling block' to either my own children or to those who have come across my path. With gratitude I receive it and by choice seek to rectify such matters in your name. Amen.

Reflection/ Action: I think I will begin to do _____ _____ as an expression of my new attitude towards children.

Day 5

Be On the Lookout

Reading: Ezekiel 34:1-16

Key verse: *Come, let us bow down in worship, let us kneel before the Lord our Maker; for he is our God and we are the people of his pasture, the flock under his care.* Psalm 95:6,7

It's so easy to be engrossed in what you are doing that events around you are unnoticed. We all can recount such incidents in relation to children who are under our feet one moment, then, we get involved in something only to realise the child is out of sight. Alarm bells in the heart and mind ring loud and long. They are not silenced until the child is seen, safe and sound.

In the parable of the lost sheep we discern a progression in Jesus' teaching: 'See that you do not look down on one of these little ones.' (Matthew 18:10). The Lord uses a child to teach His disciples, and us, three important attitudes. These were humility, the value of a child, and do not despise even a child who has been wayward.

"What do you think? If a man owns a hundred sheep, and one of them wanders away, will he not leave the ninety-nine on the hills and go and look for the one that wandered off? And if he finds it, I tell you the truth, he is happier about that one sheep than about the ninety-nine that did not wander off. In the same way your Father in heaven is not willing that any of these little ones should be lost." (Matthew 18:12-14).

The scriptures use a metaphor for men and women as 'sheep.' There are many similarities between the silliness of sheep and our disobedience. However, there is one huge difference, among others, of course. A sheep can be rounded up against its will. A person cannot.

When a child wanders away from the things of God it is easy to be dismissive of him or her. Other things can occupy the heart and mind in the mundane things of life. By neglect, if not with words, we can too readily 'look down' on such rebellious, self serving children. Jesus likens them to wandering sheep lost in a life threatening wilderness. Such children, whatever their ages, need to be tracked down and offered an opportunity to make a fresh start. This 'tracking down' is never easy. It's costly and sometimes dangerous. In some instances these 'rescue missions' require well trained, experienced searchers whose love for the Lord gives them a heart of love expressed in concerned for the lost. Special wisdom and commitment are essential elements in approaching, reaching out to and being patient with 'the lambs' who have been abused, exploited and shunned.

The compulsion for such an enterprise is our Heavenly Father's concern for the wanderer. God isn't willing to see any person lost in time or eternity, at least without being offered the alternative of God's grace. He recorded what he would do as the Shepherd and displayed it in Jesus. Throughout the gospels are accounts where His grace conquered the wayward, the indifferent and the fallen. Similar stories are being recorded in Heaven even now because He is doing it today through His under-shepherds. These are men and women serving under the Lord Jesus who is the Great Shepherd. If Heaven was in our time zone, I think there would be an everyday 'party' amongst the angels. As children are found, prodigals come home, the spiritually dead are given new life, the unrighteous are made holy, the self righteous throw off their rags and put on the garments of true righteousness woven and supplied by Jesus!

The Lord invites us, indeed, calls us to be part of His search party especially for the lost children. The first step begins with a heart that longs for them to know the Lord and Saviour, and find in Him their joy and hope. You cannot look down on those you love. To love the unlovely however and not despise them requires the heart of Jesus pulsating within. Nothing less will prevail. Nothing more is available. It is only available from Christ.

Prayer: For those called by you to the special mission of rescuing your 'lambs' from physical, moral, spiritual and intellectual danger I would lift them to you Eternal God. Watch over them and be their shield and encourager I pray. Amen.

Reflection/ Action: I will make it my business to research a Christian enterprise working on behalf of children. My intention will be to _____!

Day 6

Children of the Childless

Reading: Isaiah 54:1-5

Key verse: *Here am I, and the children God has given me.*

Hebrews 2:13

From out of His experience, Jesus makes a promise to those denied either intimate companionship or progeny. Insight into this promise flows from Isaiah 53. Here is recorded the Servant of Yahweh taking upon Himself the role of the sacrificial lamb. In verse 10 we read, '… though the Lord makes his life a guilt offering, he will see his offspring and prolong his days…'

Jesus was single. He had friends, though no intimate relationship. Children He loved, yet was father to none. Through His sacrificial, substitutionary sacrifice, the Lord gave His redeeming and resurrection life to all who put their trust in Him. The cross made it possible for Jesus to have spiritual offspring.

In Matthew 19:12, the Lord acknowledged that there would be some disciples who would remain single. Any number of reasons causing, or leading to, such a status could be listed. The wonder in the mind of the hearers was that such people were not excluded from fulfilling an effective ministry within the Kingdom of God. In fact, their singleness or childlessness, when devoted to God, becomes an unparalleled opportunity.

In city slums, suburban ghettos, isolated villages, children, and others, are being cared for in the Name of Jesus. Many of these carers are single, usually women. Their mother's heart however, will not be denied. To the disadvantaged, neglected, forsaken, or bereft children such a woman becomes 'mum.' Within her shadow there is safety, warmth, hope. She is there because of the redeeming love of Jesus. From the fulfilment of Isaiah 53 this lady raises spiritual offspring unto the Lord. For her, the words of Isaiah 54:1 become both a song of joy and a badge of honour: 'Sing, O barren woman, you who never bore a child; burst into song, shout for joy, you who were never in labour; because more are the children of the desolate woman than of her who has a husband,' says the Lord'.

For the childless couple the same holds true. To paraphrase a response of Jesus which the above couple could easily quote, 'behold, my sons and daughters which the Lord has given me!'

There are various ways by which children in need can know the tender care of a servant of the Lord. Such compassion may be face to face, or across distances. Child sponsorship through a Christian organisation offers a unique opportunity for all to be a parent, an elder brother or sister, to someone around the corner, or across the globe.

Life is unfair. Those denied an intimate relationship or of progeny can rise above it without rancour through walking by faith with Jesus. Those who are robbed of mother, father, or relatives even, can discern that unfairness fading away because of the grace of Jesus. For it is in the service of the Lord such unfairness is overruled through bringing the two together. The cross transforms unfairness into sacred ground on which there will be children to the childless, a parent for the orphan. Such faithful servants and fortunate children have this promise from the Lord: 'I (the Lord) will give them an everlasting name that will not be cut off.' (Isaiah 56:5).

Prayer: My heart is crushed by the images of the orphans of the world neglected or scavenging to survive. Father of the fatherless comfort them in their distress and raise up spiritual parents, physical guardians for these special children of your heart.

Reflection/ Action: Is the Lord impressing on my spirit the challenge to answer my own prayer?

Day 7

From the Lips of Children

Reading: Psalm 8

Key verse: *(When) '...the chief priests and teachers of the law saw the wonderful things he (Jesus) did and the children shouting in the temple area, 'Hosanna to the Son of David,' they were indignant.'*
Matthew 21:15

Children have a guileless way of saying things. There is no spitefulness when they tell you what they think, repeat or desire. We can all reach back into our memories and recall children's sayings which made us, laugh, or even cringe, and take stock of our own words and actions.

In Psalm 8 we read of the lips of children and infants being the means of praise and guileless confrontation: 'From the lips of children and infants you have ordained praise because of your enemies, to silence the foe and the avenger.' (v.2).

As with many of the psalms, this one vibrates with Messianic overtones. We know this from the account in Matthew 21. Jesus had just finished riding into Jerusalem on the donkey amidst the acclaim of the excited Passover pilgrims. He made His way to the temple area possibly to teach, maybe to worship, or as we can read, with the aim of purging the temple's precincts. What a commotion the Lord caused. Why wasn't He accosted, prevented, even arrested? Possibly because what the buyers and sellers were doing was illegal in such an area.

Where did Jesus sit in the temple? We don't know. This we do know, the lame and the blind came to Him and found healing. Such people had been excluded from the Temple services, now, perhaps for the first time they could participate in the Passover experience. Surrounded by the needy,

Jesus, to the chorus of shouting children, was confronted by grumpy and indignant priests and teachers of the Law. What had upset them? Was it the overthrow of the trading tables? No! The children's shouting 'Hosanna to the Son of David!' was the problem. These children had picked up on the acclaim of the crowd from the street procession and were joyfully repeating it. These Jewish leaders were no fools, they knew the implications undergirding all that had taken place. They simply refused to believe their own Scriptures, or apply them to this insignificant Rabbi from Nazareth. The squeals, shouts and laughter of the children became the final 'straw'.

Jesus rises to the defence of the children and infants by quoting verse two of Psalm 8. In so doing, the Lord reveals two precious insights into this Psalm. It is Messianic. The context in Matthew shows the psalm to be God's way of dealing with the enemies of the Messiah. The praise from children's lips shatters the arguments of the Messiah's opponents.

Matthew then simply says, 'He left them…'

I imagine the priests and teachers of the Law watching him go with anger in their eyes, embarrassment on their cheeks and silence on the gaping mouth. Accompanying Jesus as He left, were the children. They had played an unconscious yet profound role in the fulfilment of Scripture. I wonder how many, in later years, became disciples of the Messiah? How doubly precious to their memory would have been what they had shouted and seen on that day in the Temple.

Prayer: For the privilege of a childhood in a land influenced by the Gospel and its effect on me I give you praise. May I teach children to know you Lord Jesus. Amen.

Reflection/ Action: Were you fortunate as a child to attend Children's Church or Sunday School? Did you enjoy the stories of Jesus and sing songs to and about Him? Have you matured in your faith where songs and studies are the backdrop for being His witness?

Day 8

The Heart's Key

Reading: Deuteronomy 6:1-12

Key verse: *'As for me and my household, we will serve the Lord.'*
Joshua 24:15b

They were on the edge of a new world. Before them was land to possess, promises to see fulfilled, potential to unleash. The potential must have appeared unlimited to individuals, to families, to the embryonic nation.

With great opportunities there are also great and seductive dangers. Moses was well aware of this. As he prepares to relinquish his leadership to Joshua, he takes the nation back into an understanding of their Covenant with Yahweh. The book of Deuteronomy is a restatement of their unique relationship and calling. Within it Moses presents incentives and warnings. The obedience of faith will secure the blessings and guard against the curses.

Into the nation's heart the servant of the Lord places the key that will unlock the blessings. At the same time it will also be a sword to guard against the dangers lurking in prosperity and the immoral lifestyles of the inhabitants. The key to successfully handling the situation was to place in the heart, 'The commands, decrees and laws of the Lord.' (Deut.6:1)

Into their keeping was a 'State of Heaven' principle. Moses told them, 'these commandments that I give you today are to be upon your hearts. Impress them on your children…' (Deut. 6:6, 7) Why? So the children would enjoy long life, fear the Lord, serve Him and prosper. In this manner they would also be a testimony to the grace and wisdom of Yahweh and His Law.

Such a transferable principle was not left to chance, to occasional religious observances or to specially trained teachers. It was to be the parents' privilege. The children's mother and father became, and still remain, the Lord's primary 'Key carriers and the ones responsible to give it to the Children.' The parents were to share with their offspring, personal experiences of the Lord's dealings and faithfulness. Such openness would supplement the accounts written in the Scriptures. They also have a more personal and lasting appeal to the child.

How were they to do this? Through talking with them at home; sharing with them on the journey; showing personal reverence to God as the day ends as well as at its beginning. This isn't being religious. It's being spiritually natural, unpretentious in lifestyle and language. The climax of all this would come, for the nation of Israel, at Passover. This yearly festival was specifically designed to remind all about God's redeeming grace. At the family meal the youngest child would ask about the significance of what they were doing. The father's response would have been validated in the heart and mind of the child from all he/she had witnessed from the father or grandfather, mother or grandmother and other adults during the year. By such means a ritual was transformed into a personal covenantal relationship. This in turn prepared the heart of the child to receive 'the key which was also a sword.'

'(Yahweh) decreed His statutes for Jacob and established the law in Israel, which He commanded our forefathers to teach their children, so the next generation would know them, even the children yet to be born, and they in turn would tell their children. Then they would put their trust in God and would not forget His deeds but would keep His commands.' (Psalm 78:5-7).

Prayer: Holy Spirit I would ask you in the words of Psalm 139:23, 24 to 'Search me, O God, and know my heart; test me and know my anxious thoughts. See if there is any offensive way in me, and lead me in the way everlasting.' Amen.

Reflection/ Action: What impression of God would a child gain from observing my lifestyle, hearing my conversation and watching the way I relate to all types of people?

Day 9

Crowns, Bestowed by Grandchildren

Reading: Psalm 128

Key verse: *Children's children are a crown to the aged, and parents are the pride of their children.*   Proverbs 17:6

God has no grandchildren.

This is solely the privilege of the descendents of Adam and Eve. Within the framework of the marriage covenant, enacted in the Garden of Eden, are woven special blessings and responsibilities. Faithfulness and righteousness, especially within the marital relationship, build a foundation for security, satisfaction and spiritual formation for any children they may have.

'From everlasting to everlasting the Lord's love is with those who fear Him and His righteousness with their children's children – with those who keep His covenant and remember to obey His precepts.' (Psalm 103:17, 18)

'Blessed are all who fear the Lord, who walk in His ways...May the Lord bless you from Zion all the days of your life; may you live to see your children's children.' (Psalm 128:1, 5, 6)

In many parts of the world even today there is no certainty of enjoying the expected three score and ten years life span. In ancient times this was especially true. The Psalmist and the writer of Proverbs see a special blessing from God in granting a man or woman the privilege of seeing grandchildren. In the Western world today we take 'age' as our right and if fortunate, to see grandchildren, even great-grandchildren.

How children estimate their parents or how grandchildren see their grandparents more often than not arises out of an inheritance: 'A good man leaves an inheritance for his children's children.' (Proverbs 13:22).

Unfortunately this is usually acquainted with money. If that was all, then no poor parent could leave any inheritance to pass down the genealogical line. No! Inheritance embraces values, self esteem, trust, happy and fulfilled memories, faith, hope, love, truth, righteousness, and support for future ventures.

Parents have a wonderful privilege to flavour the lives of their children. Proverbs 17:6b says that parents who so flavour their children 'are the pride of their children.'

There is more, wonderfully more. Grandparents who invest into their children and grandchildren the flavours of faith, hope and love wear a special crown. This crown is more precious than any a mere king has ever worn. It is invisible, yet so tangible to the heart and mind. Proverbs 17:6a says it well, 'Children's children are a crown to the aged.'

Every parent and guardian should consciously, deliberately, patiently, plan to make their children proud of them. This attitude of the heart is available to any parent and guardian regardless of social status or environmental circumstances. From the Scripture's perspective this attitude of the heart flourishes from a loving fear of the Lord. This is the beginning of wisdom. In raising children and leaving an inheritance for the children's children, godly wisdom is an ongoing requirement with lifelong benefits to the grandparents, parents and children. Reading the book of Proverbs is a profitable way to keep supplementing your own wisdom.

Prayer: Prevent my joy in knowing your love Heavenly Father from robbing you of your reverence. Let your wisdom prevail in my life so I can be a blessing to others, especially the children in my sphere of influence. Amen.

Reflection/ Action: What deliberate plans have you in mind to provide an unfading and incorruptible inheritance to your children or to those entrusted to your care?

Day 10

Preparing the Child for Life

Reading: 1 Samuel 1:1-28

Key verse: *Train up a child in the way he should go, and when he is old he will not turn from it.*   Proverbs 22:6

We read the word 'train' and often our minds imagine soldierly discipline or circus training of animals. Unfortunately such an attitude simply produces unthinking robots of flesh or performance based, applause seeking adults.

The Hebrew word is elsewhere translated 'dedicate.' In Deuteronomy 20:5 it is used in dedicating a new house and 1 Kings 8:63 it refers to dedicating the temple.

Parents are encouraged to set apart their child/children according to the way he or she should go. This preferably is something that is done even before conception. Such was the case for Hannah. She cried unto the Lord for a child. Her promise was that the son she received from the Lord would be given back to Him. This is dedication. Hannah was walking in the ways of the Lord in the midst of a corrupt and disobedient society. Her example as well as her prayers helped set the course for Samuel. He also walked according to the Law of the Lord.

Proverb 22:6 can become an unfortunate mantra of superstition or pious wishful thinking. History is saturated by accounts of men and women from godly homes who walked and played in the Devil's playground. Some, by God's grace have found repentance and come back to or entered for the first time into a relationship with Jesus. Some did not. Therefore, how should we understand the implications of this Proverb?

This proverb must embrace a wider meaning than a person's spiritual experience. It's also greater than educational or moral training, important as these are. Surely it takes us beyond cultural, racial and other limitations. The writer who quotes these words wants to reach across time and country with an insight into the child as a person. He or she is not an object of a parent's fantasy, a means to have a personal ambition realised or to gain social recognition.

To dedicate or train the child could well be to unlock his or her abilities and personality within an understanding and accepting home life. This would free up the child to develop his or her inherent and often latent talents. In turn this produces a strong sense of gratitude from the child to the parents and lays a foundation for self-esteem as well as a healthy personality into maturity. There is no better environment for this to take place than in a God honouring, Scripture believing husband and wife union. Outside the home various 'masks' may have to be worn for the sake of others or discretion, these are not needed at home, or they should not be if it's a healthy and happy place. The child in such a setting knows he is loved for whom he is, and that love is unconditional.

Prayer: May you help me Sovereign Lord to discern the potential in a child's life regardless of his or her apparent limitations! I seek your grace and patience to handle frustrations and disappointments so the child will not be discouraged in becoming the man or woman you have in mind. Amen.

Reflection/Action. Do I have a clear understanding of the way I desire the child in my care to go? Is it the way the Lord would be pleased to endorse as it is in step with His Word?

Day 11

Consequences

Reading: Proverbs 1:1-19

Key verse: *Better the little that the righteous have than the wealth of many wicked; for the power of the wicked will be broken, but the Lord upholds the righteous.* Psalm 37: 16, 17

Proverbs records insights found to be true through experience. The collector of these sayings seems to want us to learn how to live a fulfilled life by learning from the wisdom and folly of others. In many ways the book is a contrast between, 'the wise' and 'the foolish,' the 'righteous' and 'the wicked.'

This book of sayings has a strong emphasis on relationships, especially in a family. There is an undercurrent of concern for the welfare of children and young people and a father's responsibility for them.

Every generation is faced with making choices which will have flow on effects. Fathers often move in their work areas and play realms confronted with those who succeed, sometimes through unethical means. The temptation is there to succumb to the same processes. Proverbs 20:7 short circuits temptation's influence, 'The righteous man leads a blameless life; blessed are his children after him.'

To look into your children's eyes and see them glow with love, respect and happiness is worth the price in walking away from the unethical and immoral. Unfortunately, some imagine they can hide their corrupt or suspect dealings and enjoy the favour of family and community. Law courts and newspapers abound with accounts of such behaviour being found out. I wonder what the eyes of the children say when they look at their father? 'The memory of the righteous will be a blessing, but the name of the wicked will rot.' (Proverbs 10:7)

Proverbs 20:7 isn't saying that the righteous man is perfect. To be righteous under the old covenant was to walk in step with the Mosaic Law. It didn't mean he never made mistakes. When he tripped up he claimed forgiveness through the tabernacle/temple sacrificial system. 'Though a righteous man falls seven times, he rises again,' (Proverbs 24:16). Through repentance and restitution he became blameless in God's sight. Notice he was blameless, not unblemished. There has ever only been one unblemished, His name is Jesus. The blameless man has his scars although he has been forgiven. From out of forgiveness he is called to forgive others. He was lifted up from his fall so that in turn he would be tender to those who trip over. Is it any wonder that his children were considered blessed!

This book places a heavy stress on righteous living. The consequences of such a life style go beyond what others might consider limiting factors on fun or ambition. For it has to be admitted that many times there is a price to pay in a corrupt society for living an ethical, spiritual and moral life. To know the favour of God and His pleasure is personally priceless. To know your family admires as well as loves you more than compensates for any temporal loss. It's also helpful to know the attitude of God as He contemplates the righteous and unrighteous. 'The Lord's curse is on the house of the wicked, but He blesses the home of the righteous. The wise inherit honour, but fools He holds up to shame.' (Proverbs 3:33, 35.) You can make the choices but before you do, weigh the consequences for your own life and its affect upon your family and faith.

Prayer: Lord I thank you for your uplifting hand. I often stumble if not outwardly then inwardly but you still reach out to me and lift me up to try again. Amen.

Reflection/ Action: If God was to 'stamp' a word on my life's report card at this moment what do I think it would be?_____

Day 12

A Poor Boy's Gift

Reading: John 6:1-15

Key verse: *Now to him who is able to do immeasurably more than all we ask or imagine, according to his power that is at work within us, to him be glory in the church and in Christ Jesus throughout all generations, for ever and ever! Amen.* Ephesians 3:20, 21

When I read the Gospels I sometimes feel a little cheated. There are so many incidental features not highlighted or followed through that leave my imagination wanting more information. Take the feeding of the 5,000 men, plus women and children, as an example.

This is the only miracle that finds its way into the four Gospels. However, while each one fills out the others in some manner, only John mentions the young boy. Why? We could very well get a little clue from his later letters? In them we read his affectionate term of 'dear children' as well as his interest in the 'chosen lady and her children.'

What arrested John's attention after Andrew had brought the boy out of the crowd and introduced him to Jesus? Was it the poverty of his appearance? We realise the boy's situation by the food in his possession. Barley bread, more in the shape of a pancake than our loaves, and two small salted fish point to his circumstances. I'm amazed the boy hadn't eaten them long before this approaching evening hour. Had he been so enthralled by Jesus the idea of eating never crossed his mind?

What did Jesus say to the child? Can you imagine the tenderness of voice and the loving look the Master offered the boy? Once again the Lord accepts the gift, so meagre, so inadequate, as though it was a priceless work of art. As Andrew expressed it, 'how far will they go among so many?' Jesus began to show Andrew and the others the grace of God in accepting, and His power in ministering it.

When the unnamed child reached home can you imagine his excitement? What words would have poured out of his lips. 'Without me Jesus could not have performed a miracle. Without my lunch hundreds and hundreds of people would have had nothing to eat.' I think people would have been dismissive of this poor child until witnesses of the event came to his support.

Did he go to Jerusalem with his father for the Passover? How shattered he must have been to see the person who broke the bread and fishes nailed to a cross. After the resurrection of Jesus, as the news spread, did it reach the ears of this boy? I like to think he jumped around yelling, 'I knew it! I knew it!' and sometime later he joins the disciples of Christ.

The saying of Jesus mentioned in Acts 20:35, 'it is more blessed to give than to receive' was highly unlikely to have been said at the feeding of the five thousand men. However the truth is certainly applicable. Was the boy reluctant in presenting it to Jesus? Probably! He did however learn a life changing lesson that still teaches today. In the wisdom of the Holy Spirit we know not the child's name. If we did someone may have made him the saint of barley and small fishes. However, he has been read about, preached about and I guess, envied, for two thousand years.

Prayer: My Lord and my God, I do not offer to you a talent, ability or money as a substitute for giving you myself. Compared to others I may not be as clever, wise and adventurous but you can have me 'lock, stock and barrel'. Amen.

Reflection/ Action: Do I tend to excuse my self from stewardship of my resources because they appear small and I'd feel embarrassed by them being known? What can I learn from this boy's gift? _____

Day 13

Molech

Reading: Leviticus 2:1-5

Key verse: *You shall have no other gods before me.*

Exodus 20:3

There are some grotesque caricatures of the eternal God. The rebellious heart and mind of Humankind has made a mockery of the Creator/Redeemer. All a person has to do is compare the idols of paganism to the revelation of God in the Scriptures to grasp that fact.

In the Judeo-Christian Scriptures is mentioned an abomination called Molech. He was one of the gods of the Canaanites about which the Israelite nation was warned. Devotees of this god sacrificed children to it for favourable treatment and good harvests. Across the centuries and in various cultures this devilish practice has taken place. Today, in so called Christianized countries, child sacrifice happens in a less crude and bloody way. Molech receives its offering today on the altar of greed, lust, ambition and selfishness.

The Lord God, Yahweh, has placed on record His loathing of the cult of child sacrifice, in any form. In His Word we are confronted by the Lord's indignation against those who so abuse children. 'I will set my face against that man and I will cut him off from his people; for by giving his children to Molech, he has defiled my sanctuary and profaned my holy name.' Leviticus 20:3.

Whenever a parent or guardian violates the integrity and person of a child God is dishonoured, His Name profaned. Why? For a couple of reasons! One relates to the creation of Humankind. Genesis chapter 1 specifically declares that Adam and Eve were made in the image of God.

Even when Sin made a breach between the Lord God and Humankind, it could not erase the image. Twist it, yes! Defile it, yes! Deny it, no! A second reason is seen in Yahweh's role as Redeemer. He claims the first born for His own in a special relationship. Every child is precious to Him! However the firstborn in scripture has a meaning pointing beyond itself to Jesus as 'The Firstborn from the dead.' Every child is consecrated to Him although the firstborn had that symbolism of a future event. No child is to be sacrificed to any form of Molech! He or she is to be sanctified and redeemed in the Biblical faith through a substitutionary offering. There is a lot of meaning and typology in this which finds fulfilment in Jesus and His death on the cross.

The Psalmist was compelled to write that sons are a heritage from the Lord, children a reward from Him. (Ps.127:3) Treating a child as evolutionary junk; making an unwanted baby expendable; manipulating boys and girls for personal profit; corrupting and thereby destroying the young is an attack on the Lord's heritage and reward. God takes it personally!

Again we have to ask, why?

Because God's very nature is Holiness and Love. His very being is profaned by such anti-God attitudes and behaviour. If such an abuser enters His sanctuary, it is polluted. (Lev. 20:3). All of us need to remember that God is a jealous God. He is jealous for His Name; for His creation; for His Word; for His people; and I believe, especially for babies and children.

The safest legacy for any child is having parents who are faithful in obedience to Jesus Christ. This salvation relationship is meant to provide a refuge for any child from the 'Molechs' of this world. Fortunate is the boy or girl growing up with parents or guardians under the 'umbrella' of Christ's word and Spirit. They realise they are precious to God as well as to their parents.

Prayer: This is my longing Lord, expressed in your own words, 'Consecrate yourselves and be holy, because I am the Lord your God.

Keep my decrees and follow them. I am the Lord, who makes you holy.' Leviticus 20:7, 8. Amen.

Reflection/ Action: What are some of the 'Molechs' our modern society has erected to the moral, physical and spiritual death of children? How may I be God's protector of these innocents? _____
_____

Day 14

Against the Odds

Reading: Acts 16:1-5, 2 Timothy 1:3-7

Key verse: *It gave me great joy to have some brothers come and tell me about your faithfulness to the truth and how you continue to walk in the truth. I have no greater joy than to hear that my children are walking in the truth.* 3 John 3, 4

The odds were against him. He was of mixed racial parentage. He had to grow up straddling two cultures, Greek and Jewish. Timid by nature he probably had difficult times from the neighbourhood children. Timothy however stands out in secular and sacred literature and history as among the finest of disciples.

Life is unfair, often cruel, to a growing child. For a boy in Timothy's situation the added burdens could have infected his personality with bitterness, anger and spitefulness. This didn't happen. What we read about him depicts him as one who earned the respect of his elders and was found faithful in the duties assigned to him.

Certain features emerge from a study of Timothy. These should be an encouragement to any God honouring parent in an unequally yoked marital and spiritual relationship. Boys and girls living within a mixed racial and cultural family in the midst of unsympathetic neighbours, can also have hope.

A fulfilled life for Timothy stemmed from his mother and grandmother's devout faith. Eunice, the mother, would not have found it easy. Being Jewish she would have desired her son to be circumcised and celebrate Bar Mitzvah. The inference from this lack points to hostility from the pagan husband/father. Here was a boy caught between two worlds.

The fact that he matured into a man unscarred by this must be attributed as 2 Timothy 3:15 puts it to the fact 'how from infancy you have known the holy Scriptures, which are able to make you wise for salvation through faith in Christ Jesus.' Eunice and Lois's unfeigned faith would have backed up the Scriptures. Around the heart and mind of a growing boy the teaching, the lifestyle, the prayers of these two women would have built a sense of security and identity no outside prejudice or arrows of bitterness could breach.

When the apostle Paul came to Timothy's town the Gospel was proclaimed. It created a furore. Paul and Barnabas were assaulted, leaving the apostle, as the crowd thought, dead. He wasn't! Recovering his 'breath' he returned with Barnabas to the town before moving on. Some time later Paul returns to the town, this time with Silas. What do they discover? Timothy, his mother and grandmother are disciples of Christ. They are active within the Christian fellowship so much so that the leaders of the local churches spoke very highly of Timothy. Not only had he found the fulfilment of the Jewish Scriptures, he also realised the significance of his name. Timothy means, 'worshipping or honouring God.'

Knowing his own worth in the sight of God gave Timothy the dignity, strength and humility to weather any sarcasm and scorn. What Paul wrote about Timothy is a remarkable reference. Some of the credit must go back to his mother and grandmother. This is what was written, 'I have no one else like him, who takes a genuine interest in your welfare…you know that Timothy has proved himself, because as a son with his father he has served with me in the work of the gospel.' (Philippians 2:21, 22)

Prayer: So many I know of Lord Jesus do not have Timothy's advantage in their growing up. Ignorance of you and your word, even in religious circles is frightening and harming the young. O God, may your Word penetrate such homes and raise up more like Timothy I pray. Amen.

Reflection/ Action: Your Word is life and light to the heart of young and old, how may I introduce someone to it today? Can I open your Word to the mind of another so they might hear your voice and know your will? Could it be _____?

Day 15

The 'O' Word

Reading: Deuteronomy 10:12-21

Key verse: *Not everyone who says to me 'Lord, Lord,' will enter the kingdom of heaven, but only he who does the will of my Father who is in Heaven.* Matthew 7:21

Something within our personality struggles against the 'O' word. However you describe the source of the resistance it's rooted in our self-will. From birth this abhorrence of Obedience is evident. It walks with us all our life. We cope with it through various ways, sullenly, gladly, indifferently.

An interesting feature of 'O' comes from its association with hearing. In Young's concordance the Hebrew word 'Shamea' gives us a framework for understanding the significance of the 'O' word. Adam, after he had eaten the forbidden fruit heard (shamea) the voice of God in the Garden. The trouble was that Adam had not obeyed (shamea) what God had commanded. (Genesis 2:16, 17) Ever since that time, the descendents of Adam and Eve have suffered from a similar 'deafness.' When we put the two verses side by side we realise, to hear is to obey.

Reading Ephesians 6:1, we understand that children are expected to obey their parents. Once again we notice there is another link between hearing and obeying. The Greek word, hupakoe comes from 'hupo' under, plus 'akouo' to hear. Obedience therefore is hearing and choosing to respond.

In the Decalogue the 5th commandment is for children, of all ages, to honour their parents. Attached to this was 'so that you may live long and that it may go well with you in the land…'

Quite motivational. Don't you agree?

In the New Testament the reason for obedience is due to a relationship with Jesus as Lord. A child is also to honour his/her parents for reasons mentioned above. This is sometimes hard. Not all parents are honourable either in their life style or the way they treat their children. However, God's word does expect us as children, to honour our parents, even the unworthy ones. A comparison may enlighten. The Roman Caesars gave the Church a hard time in the first couple of centuries of the Christian era. The Caesars were murderous, brutal and immoral. However, when Peter wrote to the suffering Church he told them 'honour the king (Caesar)' (1 Peter 2:17). The man was not honourable but the position he held, was. The same attitude must apply to parents.

The era in which the New Testament was written, Caesar and a child's father exercised life and death over their charges. In some countries, and religions, this still applies. Once again, quite motivational!

However, there is a higher call on the child. When the Gospel is heard it calls for a personal commitment to Jesus Christ. It's a call to reverse the attitude and actions of Adam in the garden. To hear and to obey has its rewards and responsibilities. To accept the offer of Jesus as Lord and Saviour may well cause offence to family, culture, or religion. That could be life threatening. Jesus is on record as saying that some may have to pay such a price. As Peter and John said before the Sanhedrin, 'we must obey God rather than men.'

The 'O' word for all of us has a price tag. In responding to it, from our Lord's perspective, there is also great blessing and future glory. Quite motivational don't you agree?

Prayer: Deliver me from being a theorist about your word Lord Jesus. I want to be a doer of your word, putting into practice what you place on my heart as I read the scriptures for I want to know your blessing, not your disappointment. Amen.

Reflection/ Action: What aspect of 'O' have I been avoiding?

Day 16

Some Children Do Have Them

Reading: Ephesians 3:1-21

Key verse: *We have heard with our ears, O God; our fathers have told us what you did in their days, in days long ago.* Psalm 44:1

It's easy to father a child. It's much harder to be a father to the child. There is a combination of awesome privilege and demanding responsibility to wear the title, 'father.' Where can a man go to learn how to be a dad? To whom can he look as a suitable mentor for the role and relationship he must exercise?

Ephesians 3:14, 15 is the answer. '...I kneel before the Father, from whom His whole family in heaven and earth derives its name.' The word translated 'family' can also be translated 'fatherhood.' Therefore a man, especially a Christian man, can base his approach to fatherhood from an understanding of God as revealed in the Old and New Testaments. Paul's vivid description of kneeling before the Father of glory was to pray that his readers might know the power, the love, the fellowship and the fullness of God. This is where success as a father begins, on a man's knees.

Later in his letter, Paul stresses a couple of practical matters as pointers for Christian fathers. It must always be remembered that many converts to Christ came out of pagan backgrounds. Being a faithful, gracious, 'hands on dad' was a new world to be explored. 'Fathers, do not exasperate your children; instead, bring them up in the training and instruction of the Lord.' (Ephesians 6:4)

The word Paul uses has the force of so pressurising the child, probably verbally, that the boy or girl becomes disheartened and discouraged.

When writing to the Church at Colosse he challenges the dads not to embitter their children and so see them become emotional, spiritual or relational 'drop-outs.' (Colossians 3:21)

That warning of the negative is quickly overtaken by a positive statement. 'Bring them up in the training and instruction of the Lord.' This must be something like; 'Son, what you see in me, how I honour the Lord, desire to know His word, and put it into practice, I want you to copy.' For a child to rise to this calling requires the father's love, wisdom, investment, perseverance and discipline.' The father's ability to provide this will flow from his personal experience of knowing it from his heavenly Father.

> It's easy to give a child some money,
> priceless, however to give him your time.
> It's easy to verbally belittle a child,
> princely however to encourage her.
> It's easy to react negatively to a child,
> therapeutic to bless with the positive.
> It's easy to crush a child's self image,
> beautiful when you allow it to bloom.
> It's easy to raise barriers to a child's faith,
> eternally precious to see faith birthed.

Being a father is a wonderful privilege not enjoyed by all men. Such an honour also carries the burden of accountability especially for the formative years and outlook of the child. Let God's word shape your understanding and the Spirit of God mould you according to the nature of your heavenly Father.

Prayer: Make me in your image whether I'm a father or mother physically or spiritually. Let your heart rule my mind and guide my behaviour and attitude so my children will have an incentive to know and serve you. Amen.

Reflection/ Action: As God is my role model as a father how well do I know Him? Does my life cast shadows of His personality over my family?

Day 17

A Parent's Joy

Reading 2 John

Key verse: *Dear children, keep yourself from idols.* 1 John 5:21

As the babe grows, family and friends wait expectantly for his, or her, first steps. There is something exciting, joyously so, in watching the little one let go of 'the prop' and take a faltering, stumbling step. It doesn't matter how many children belong to your family, the joyousness of each occasion never diminishes.

Those first hesitant steps begin a life of discovery, duty, delight, danger, discipline. The physical steps are mirrored in the unseen realm of the moral and spiritual. In coming years that which is unseen works it way out into the seen. The way the adult of later life 'walks' will be guided not by the shoes he/she wears but by the set of the heart. Many are the influences which bear down on a child's heart. The importance of faithful, prayerful, loving parents in protecting their child's heart and instilling the principles of truth cannot be exaggerated.

The apostle John in writing two of his letters penned his joy about hearing how his 'children' walked. These children would have been those who had come to faith in Jesus Christ under his ministry. Undoubtedly, most of those mentioned were mature people, yet to the aged John, they were his 'children in the faith.' He writes 'It has given me great joy to find some of your children walking in the truth, just as the Father commanded us.' (2 John 4). In the third letter, this time to a friend Gaius, he wrote, 'I have no greater joy than to hear that my children are walking in the truth.'

The source of his joy was to hear that the 'children' were walking, continuing, in the truth. Surely this is the longing of Christian parents. Why? For truth is the foundation of freedom. It is the character of Jesus. Truth is the nature of God. It is the testimony of His word. Without truth, love would be called into question. Without Truth there could be no absolutes, and so no certainties in faith or relationships.

Learning to walk is filled with falls, bruises, tears, frustration as well as delight. Determination is the key. The unknown calls to be explored for all children. What is ahead is unknown for children and adults. Encouragement and support by parents and others helps the child, and of course older folk, to get up after a fall and keep walking into the unknown. The spiritual implications are self evident. As parents walk in 'the way the truth and the life' they will leave invisible footprints in the heart of their child/children. As parents heed the invitation of Jesus to 'come follow me' there will be great joy for them to watch their child/children put his/her feet into those 'footprints' and follow the Lord. There is perhaps no greater example to be set for a child than to see his or her parent not simply talking the walk, but walking the calling. Paul said it to his spiritual children in Philippians 4:9, ' Whatever you have learned or received or heard from me, or seen in me – put it into practice. And the God of peace will be with you.'

Prayer: Lord, are you satisfied with my 'walk' so far? I know I get weary sometimes as the going gets tough or monotonous, but your Spirit and Word inspire me to press on. O God, help me help my children to walk and not grow weary in your path for them. Amen.

Reflection/ Action: The prophet Amos reminds me that two can only walk together if they are in agreement. (Amos 3:3) I appreciate your graciousness in matching my pace, but in all honesty Lord, am I in step with you?

Day 18

Hidden Treasure

Reading: Matthew 6:19-24

Key verse: *For God, who said, 'Let light shine out of darkness,' made his light shine in our hearts to give us the light of the glory of God in the face of Christ. But we have this treasure in jars of clay to show that the all-surpassing power is from God and not from us.'*
2 Corinthians 4:6, 7

A thesaurus is not an intellectual dinosaur. It's a dictionary in which words and their 'relatives' are found. The word comes from the Greek and means, 'storehouse' 'treasury.' In the Scriptures we find Jesus and Paul using this word, usually translated 'to store up'. 'The good man brings good things out of the good stored up in him, and the evil man brings evil things out of the evil stored up in him.' (Matt.12:35)

The apostle Paul links this word in a relationship between parent and child. '…children should not have to save up (store up) for their parents, but parents for their children.' (2 Cor. 12:14b)

Notice the obligation on the parents. They are expected in the teaching of God's Word to 'save up' 'store up' to be a thesaurus, (from the Greek 'thesauros') for their children. What comes to mind when you read the word to save up, store up? Usually it is money or material things. That's important and helpful but not always possible although some inheritance may be a future possibility. There is a more pressing and important truth pressing for acceptance. Parents are responsible to bank, invest, place within the heart and mind of their God given charges moral and spiritual gems. In the course of the years this treasury builds up and gathers interest. It is from out of the treasury vault of the heart that a maturing child makes decisions, evaluates life, understands God's word and dealings, and inter-acts with others.

How does a parent go about investing eternal treasure into the life of his/herchildren? Whether you invest precious gems or rubble comes down to personal lifestyle, priorities, faith, hope, love. From the Biblical viewpoint all of this flows out of a personal walk and maturing relationship of faith in God through the Lord Jesus Christ. In effect, God quarries from within a faithful parent the jewels to be imparted to the children. These gems have been formed through a parent's life experiences, conversion, faithful testimony, growing in the grace and knowledge of Jesus. As a child watches, listens, respects, embraces his/her parents the vault is being filled. The Lord wants to transfer precious gems into the 'vault' of the child. What an indictment upon the parents if all the child collects is rubble?

A father or mother is not simply investing value into the heart and mind of their child. They have, in effect a hidden impact on future generations. There is also the outworking of the investment into the moral and spiritual tone of a home and a community. Beyond all that however, are the eternal consequences for all who are within the family circle. Ultimately what is being invested finds its way into the treasury of Heaven.

"Do not store up for yourselves treasures on earth, where moth and rust destroy, and where thieves break in and steal. But store up for yourselves treasures in heaven, where moth and rust do not destroy, and where thieves do not break in and steal. For where your treasure is, there your heart will be also." (Matthew 6:19-21)

A strange, though not surprising thing happens when parents invest their moral, intellectual, spiritual treasure into the heart and mind of their children. Parents come to find that children have returned the favour. By placing in the parents' hearts the gems of memories, gratitude, honour and untarnished love. That is priceless!

Prayer: To be your 'thesaurus' from which my children can draw godly information in their formative years is an awesome privilege and responsibility. May I never cease to receive your 'deposits' nor be closed for business to my children and any others in need. Amen.

Reflection/ Action: How well stocked am I at this moment in the wealth of Heaven? Are those seeking 'withdrawals' finding satisfaction or disappointment?

Day 19

The Garment of Love

Reading: 1 John 4:7-21.

Key verse: *'...the older women...can train the younger women to love their husbands and children,'*   Titus 2:4

In a culture of arranged marriages I can understand (as a man) the instruction for showing young wives how to show love to their husbands. (Paul instructs husbands in Ephesians 5: 25-29 on their love code. Peter adds his bit in 1 Peter 3:1-6). That which I wondered at, initially, was his advice to instruct them to love their babies and growing children. I thought that would have been so natural for a woman. On reflection however it isn't too hard to imagine reasons for a mother having difficulty in loving an unwanted, disfigured or handicapped child, especially if the husband wasn't supportive or there wasn't any love blossoming in the arranged relationship. God doesn't condone such lack of love, but offers His help to overcome it.

How can one person teach another to love?

Love must first of all be defined. It goes beyond the emotional, is greater than personal feelings of like and dislike. Love in its most basic garment is simply caring for the well being and welfare of another, especially of the vulnerable. This garment from a Christian's understanding is knitted from the Scripture's revelation of God and Humankind. Without this knowledge Human love is threadbare and merely strands of emotion that soon unravel when self interest is affected.

Love grows out of knowing God through Jesus Christ. God is Holy Love, not the sentimental, saccharine sweet emotion often portrayed in books or theatre. The ultimate portrayal of love is Calvary. We can help people to love by introducing them to the One who is Love. 'We love because He first loved us.' 1 John 4:19 expresses it so forcefully.

Love grows out of understanding the uniqueness of each individual. We have our origins in a special act of God as recorded in Genesis 1 and 2. Although Adam and Eve's rebellion has marred and scarred God's handiwork, it has not erased His imprint. Each baby bears the 'fingerprint' of God. Therefore, regardless of the child's appearance or lineage, he or she is worthy of love.

Love grows out of an act of the will. If it were simply an act of passion, love would be a roller coaster ride. However Jesus lifts love onto a stable, unshakeable footing by commanding His disciples to love. If it can be commanded, it can be responded to. Love is an act of the will, a choice beyond self interest and personal gain. The amazing fact that emerges when a man or woman chooses to obey the command, his or her heart and mind is supplied with Love's glorious garments. God honours those who honour Him through a deliberate act of obedience to His Word. This isn't to say such a choice is easy, far from it. However in taking God at His word you will find He supplies the resources to carry it through.

Whenever a mother is encouraged to love her children according to the Biblical principles so much sorrow and wasted years are averted. The garment of Love makes the unwanted, wanted; the unlovely, beautiful; the handicapped, precious!

That is what Jesus has done for each of us in His Father's sight. We were dead to God because of our indifference, rebellion and self righteousness. We were not a pretty sight. Our spiritual odour was offensive to His 'nostrils' and we were marred 'vessels' unsuitable for serving the Lord. Yet He chose to love us and set about reclaiming us. What a privilege to show this love and acceptance to others. What an honour to express it to others in His Name.

Prayer: Am I qualified Lord to be a teacher about your love? Help me to express your understanding of love to my spouse, to my children, to my relatives, to those under my protection and to be a model others can follow. Amen.

Reflection/ Action: How well dressed am I in the garment of God's love? Do I wear it well in my relationship with my nearest and dearest? Am I in need of a re-fitting?

Day 20

A Child's An Indicator of a Father's Suitability

Reading: Psalm 128

Key verse: *My son (daughter), give me your heart and let your eyes keep to my ways.* Proverbs 23:26

Every Christian man should aspire to be an Elder in the local fellowship. In essence the Biblical picture of an Elder is God's estimation of a spiritual gentleman. To put it perhaps more bluntly, in a very special way, an Elder is to be the reflection of Jesus before the Church and community.

1 Timothy 3:1-7 spells out some very tangible qualities for considering a man for such a responsibility. These are overlooked by any congregation to its own hurt. One such requirement is 'He must manage his own family well and see that his children obey him with proper respect.'

To be a manager comes easier to some than others. Still, it can be learnt. Being a father whose children obey and respect must also be learnt. So often a father stresses the issue of obedience to his will regardless of mitigating circumstances. When the boy or girl is young it's easy to coerce them into doing what dad says. If all else fails, there is the 'stick.' A wise father will learn that obedience stems from the will, not the outward display of conforming. Sure there will be times when a child has to be disciplined with strictness. We live in a rebellious world and it infects us all. When discipline needs to be strict, it must also be fair and therapeutic.

In considering discipline a parent, and certainly the father, needs to understand the personality and temperament of the child. The smack on the rump may direct some children into right behaviour whilst it will have no impact on others. Restriction of privileges, loss of 'free time' or refusing to allow friends over can sometimes be more effective and long lasting. This is not always easy to implement as it can make a father seem uncaring. However, it will be helpful to keep in mind the principle behind God's various ways of disciplining us. 'God disciplines us for our good, that we may share in His holiness. No discipline seems pleasant at the time, but painful. Later on, however, it produces a harvest of righteousness and peace for those who have been trained by it.' (Hebrews 12:10, 11) The aim of our Heavenly Father's discipline is to make us mature, fully developed, keen disciples. Surely we as fathers should aim for nothing less for our children.

Respect is the key to obedience in a maturing child. Essentially being a father is a journey of discovery in the company of your child. A dad takes the child from dependence to freedom; from unquestioning response to reasoning together; from example to personal practice; from doing to being; from selfish to caring about the welfare of others. On the way the child sees the integrity, the faith, the devotion of his or her dad and new dimensions blossom in the relationship. Colouring it all will be the radiance of honour and respect.

The journey a father and a child take should be seen as the highest privilege. A child spells love as 't i m e' spent with the most important people in his or her life. It is what he/she will remember long after he/she has moved away or when parents have been called into the presence of the Lord. The Church stands in urgent need of such men. May God be using fathers to aspire to this calling and at the same time inspiring their sons especially to follow suit.

Prayer: Save me dear Lord from the snares of ambition and fame, which could have a negative impact upon my children. I would like to delight in my children as you delight in your children and see the joy flow through their eyes and their hugs. Amen.

Reflection/ Action: In the scale of priorities, where do I place my children or those in my care? What have I taught them about their worth to me and their worth to their Heavenly Father?

Day 21

Beware the Phantoms of Life

Reading: 1 Corinthians 10:1-15

Key verse: *Praise be to the God and Father of our Lord Jesus Christ! In His great mercy He has given us new birth into a living hope through the resurrection of Jesus Christ from the dead.*   1 Peter 1:3

We know and understand that the apostle John was writing to more than youngsters in 1 John 5:21 when warning against idols. It was an affectionate term he used for those with whom he had shared his faith, time and ministry. In concluding his letter, John urges his readers to be on their guard against the seductive influences of their ungodly society. The Church is always surrounded by tangible and spiritual forces whose aim is to weaken and lead astray a disciple from his or her walk with Jesus Christ.

Children need protection from a whole range of moral, physical and spiritual 'idols.' Being a parent involves helping the child understand the seductive powers of an idol and being a shield behind which the child can find security and wisdom. It also means teaching and equipping the child to clothe himself/herself in God's armour to resist the allure of the 'idol.'

Children soon realise life's enemies can be more than flesh and blood. There are ideologies to face which appear harmless but have the power to corrupt mind, body and spirit. Good things used unwisely and without godly discipline can be turned into idols. This happened to Israel. God told Moses to erect a bronze pole with a serpent represented on it. All who were bitten by a serpent plague could look to it and by faith be healed. Numbers 21:4-9. Hundreds of years later, in the reign of King Hezekiah, the superstitious nature of unbelief had turned this pole into an object of worship. The king had it crushed and ground into dust. 2 Kings 18:4. How easy the soul can create 'idols' even out of acts of God's grace.

Jesus also warned against a competitor for the supreme attraction of a person's allegiance. Matthew 6:24: 'No one can serve two masters… you cannot serve both God and money.' The phantom of affluence makes itself felt through materialism. It's as much an idol as any graven image of heathen tribes. The word in the New Testament for idol means phantom or vanity. Parents must protect their children from any form of idolatry by personal example and living under the discipline of the Cross.

Success stems from understanding the meaning in the text of the word, 'keep.' It means to guard. Parents are to instruct their sons and daughters in guard duty. God has supplied the resources, His disciples must apply them, be competent with them. There's scripture, prayer, worship, the Holy Spirit, the honour of Jesus, godly mentors to name a few. In the military language of the apostle Paul in Ephesians 6, put on the whole armour of Christ. Only then will a parent, a child, keep the phantoms defeated.

The same word is used in 2 Thessalonians 3:3. This is the Lord God's promise that will be effective when His spiritual son or daughter faithfully learns to be 'on guard.' 'The Lord is faithful, and He will strengthen and protect (keep, guard) you from the evil one.' That means you have a personal responsibility to place yourself under His protection. Jude calls you and me 'Dear friends, build yourselves up in your most holy faith and pray in the Holy Spirit. Keep yourselves in God's love as you wait for the mercy of our Lord Jesus Christ to bring you to eternal life.' Jude 20, 21.

Prayer: Guard my heart and mind Beloved Lord. Captivate my attention always and leave no room for any rivals. Amen.

Reflection/Action: Are there things in my life my soul is playing around with which have the capacity of turning into a rival to my allegiance to Jesus Christ? What steps are required to make the 'idol' into 'dust?'

Day 22

A Child's Faith in Old Age

Reading: Psalm 71

Key verse: *Since my youth, O God, you have taught me, and to this day I declare your marvellous deeds.* Psalm 71:17

When a child mingles with Jesus there is almost an instant rapport. Through the gospel stories, by the power of the Holy Spirit and the personal preparation of the teacher, a boy or girl senses the presence of Jesus. Given the opportunity a child unreservedly wants to have Jesus as their friend, saviour and ultimately, Lord.

Cynics often belittle a child's faith, intentionally or otherwise, for they imagine a child is incapable of a faith response to Jesus or to any thing. Such scoffers erect barriers over which a child has to continually climb. The testimonies in old age show disciples from a young age reveal the truth of Psalm 71. 'For you have been my hope, O Sovereign Lord, my confidence since my youth. From birth I have relied upon you;' (verses 5, 6).

The unnamed Psalmist, possibly David, looks back on his childhood's faith as it has been moulded, attacked, ridiculed and faced troublesome times. His response is summed up in verses 22-24, 'I will praise you with the harp for your faithfulness, O my God; I will sing praises to you with the lyre, O Holy One of Israel. My lips will shout for joy when I sing praises to you – I, whom you have redeemed. My tongue will tell of your righteous acts all day long, for those who wanted to harm me have been put to shame and confusion.'

Teachers of children are to see themselves as stepping stones into a rendezvous with Jesus. As such, the instructions given are foundational

Truth on which the child can build his or her life as a maturing disciple. We all live in a hostile world that seeks to corrupt the ideals of youth, undermine Truth's foundation and cower the aging and vulnerable saints. The Psalmist felt this pressure. 'Even when I'm old and grey, do not forsake me, O God, till I declare your power to the next generation, your might to all who are to come.' (verse 18) Knowing the scriptures, the writer of this Psalm would cling to Yahweh's promise never to leave or forsake those who put their trust in Him. What a comfort and strength.

The child who grows up in the atmosphere of Christ has a privilege only understood in later life. He/she has been given an unfading guide for understanding life. The boy or girl has an appreciation of Truth which will protect against the corrosive effect of Satan's lies. As he/she journeys into his/her unknown future they can face it with Faith in the One who is Faithful. Fear lurks in all the doubts, unfairness and uncertainties of everyday living. A child who keeps hold of his/her Lord's hand through faith will know such fear and its companions can be 'caged'.

Most of us are not overly excited about growing old. There are undoubted negatives to it although it can have more going for it than the alternative of dying young. However, years are required to pass over you and me if we are to have a testimony concerning the person and work of the Lord Jesus within our life. The Psalmist's words could be most fitting to all in the aging process, 'I will come and proclaim your mighty acts, O Sovereign Lord; I will proclaim your righteousness, yours alone. Since my youth, O God, you have taught me, and to this day I declare your marvellous deeds.' (Verses 16, 17)

Prayer: I will praise you Lord! I will make my years tell a history of your faithfulness and forgiveness. I desire your Spirit to make me a placard for your mercy especially to the up coming generations. Amen.

Reflection/ Action: How well am I aging? What stories of God's grace, goodness and glory am I sharing with children and adults?

Day 23

When a Child Dreams

Reading: Genesis 37:2-11

Key verse: *We do not want you to become lazy, but to imitate those who through faith and patience inherit what has been promised.*
Hebrews 6:12

Joseph was a dreamer. We meet him in Genesis 37 when he is seventeen. His ten older brothers hated him due to a number of reasons, including Joseph's unfavourable report about them and he being 'father's favourite.' We don't know when he began to have dreams. This we do know, God placed them in this young man's mind for a reason that would require years of difficulties before being fulfilled. Joseph could only hold onto his dreams through knowing the One who had given them.

We all have dreams. Some are remembered, some not. They come in all 'shapes and sizes' as they emerge from our inner being in our sleep. Some dreams take hold of our consciousness and create a longing to see them fulfilled. Some, we pray, never see the light of day.

Children have their dreams. Circumstances create longings of the heart which throw pictures into the mind at night. A neglected child dreams of parental love; a deprived boy may dream of being a doctor, a girl dreams to be a teacher; a hungry child dreams of someone caring enough to ease the pain; an abused child cries for and dreams about a place of safety.

There is a sickness in the world designed to destroy the dreams of children, especially dreams that are flavoured by, or committed to God. The brothers of Joseph have their modern day counterparts. Potiphar's vindictive wife and the forgetful fellow 'prisoners' in Joseph's life have their genetic offspring on the World's stage today. (Read Genesis 39, 40). Not all dreams have satisfying outcomes like Joseph's. We have all come across young and old with shattered dreams. They carry the shattered pieces in saddened hearts or bitter spirits. I wonder if God feels let down by those who could have helped, but didn't? I believe He does. I believe also that our Lord feels the pain of those who have been failed by others. Isaiah reminds us that Yahweh 'In all their (Israel's) distress, he too was distressed' (ch.63:9).

Joseph was a dreamer. It required God's overruling purposes and His involving others in Joseph's affairs for that dream to come true. This may well be the privilege God invests in the lives of parents, guardians, friends, and in so many cases now, sponsors. Opportunities exist for us to be involved in the life of at least one child. Maybe this will be through sponsorship; maybe it will come about by involvement with an organisation committed to the total welfare of children.

The Lord God doesn't give anyone a dream for personal self importance He gives it for the welfare of others, even the welfare of those who sought to wreck the dream. Joseph put it well when he said about the outcome of his dream and treatment, 'You intended to harm me, but God intended it for good to accomplish what is now being done, the saving of many lives' (Genesis 50:20).

I doubt whether there could be a greater thrill, outside of knowing Jesus and serving Him, than having the privilege of helping a child's God directed dream materialise. Wouldn't it be awesome to hear a child say to Jesus, 'Thank you Jesus for that person (your name) through whom you blessed me and helped my dream to come true.' That child or those children will treasure your name always. The tangible nature of what you have given them will be your cause for celebration and gratitude in being a 'Dream Maker.'

Prayer: O Sovereign Redeemer, giver of dreams, let them not be like a mirage of the mind to a child or those older. Grant them the faith to await the dreams fulfilment. If it means you calling on others, including me, to make it happen, bring it about I pray. Amen.

Reflection/ Action: Can I think of someone who helped a dream or two of mine come true? Have I thanked God for them? Will someone give thanks for me for a similar reason?

Day 24

Fathers with Foresight

Reading: Proverbs 4:1-13

Key verse: *My son, preserve sound judgement and discernment, do not let them out of your sight; they will be life for you, an ornament to grace your neck.*   Proverbs 3:21, 22

Children don't have the capacity to see the inherent dangers lurking in some of their actions, their choices and their wants. From the beginning of creation the purpose of God for children was to protect them through a stable and wise family life. Humankind's rejection of Yahweh's standards and the elevation of personal preference have ushered in dangerous and deadly consequences for many children.

When Jesus calls a man unto Himself and places him as a husband and father of a family, that man has great privileges enmeshed with tremendous responsibilities. 'If anyone does not provide for his relatives, and especially for his immediate family, he has denied the faith and is worse than an unbeliever.' (1 Timothy 5:8)

The word 'provide' means 'to think beforehand.' Before the child dives into 'the water' of his interest, the father must check out what lurks beneath. Depending upon the situation, whether the child dives, wades or simply sits that one out, comes from a father's (and mother's) investigation and deliberation. If parents neglect to exercise the adult ability of thinking through a matter on behalf of their child, broken hearts and broken lives will result. Proverbs 29:15 puts it this way, 'a child left to himself disgraces his mother.'

The Scriptures are a storehouse of information that nourishes an adult's foresight faculties. We are not expected to live by 'bread' alone.

We are expected, as disciples of Jesus, to live by every word of our heavenly Father. In its pages we find examples and principles relevant to providing for our children.

Jesus gave two parables dealing with the need to think before acting, or in other words, having foresight from insight. In Luke 14:28-33 Jesus tells about a tower builder who was unable to finish the job. He also speaks of a king planning a war but unsure about having sufficient resources to win. Being His disciple required a willingness to pay the cost by thinking matters through beforehand. Such a principle also applies to making decisions as a father. Providing for the family has a cost on a man's own 'tower.' In the matter of the family it means, does the father, the mother, have the resources and ability to do their own thing without neglect to the children? The rule Jesus would have a man apply is 'how does it square up with carrying your cross?' Taking up 'one's own cross' means putting to death your own will so as to do the will of God. There is also the companion word 'deny yourself' and in the context of family surely there are times when parents must deny themselves legitimate matters for the children's sake in accordance with God's purposes.

Providing for the family goes well beyond financial security. There is providing a safe haven from the pressures of a godless world; understanding the nature, dreams, and fears of his children; leading them to confidence and faith. Locked within each breast are God given gifts and abilities needing permission and guidance to emerge. Parents are required to exercise foresight in developing a child's creative powers.

When failure comes, or rebellion, will mercy and grace be provided and prevail? It will insofar as the father and mother have tasted it from God.

A failure to provide through Love's foresight and Life's learning is an indictment on the Faith. Unbelievers scoff as they see the wounded spirits and broken hearts of the Christian couple's children. The Church will also be robbed of the mature, wholesome and creative involvement of the disillusioned, dispirited and defeated child. Let us not fail the children. Let us not rob the future of their God given gifts!

Prayer: I would like to adorn your doctrine by my life precious Lord, to wear it with pride in you and in humility express my wonder in your choosing me to belong to you. Amen.

Reflection/ Action: What 'ornaments' am I 'wearing around my neck' due to God's grace to me through others? Am I capable of being His distributor of the same to others?

Day 25

The Shepherd's Rod

Reading: Psalm 23

Key verse: *Shepherd your people with your staff, the flock of your inheritance.* Micah 7:14

I was fortunate as I grew through childhood. My parents, when they deemed it necessary, applied their hand to the seat of my pants – with me in them. I know that what I received was done out of love and for my own good. Whether mum or dad realised it (probably not) they were exercising what the Scripture calls, a shepherd's heart. That is, they had the rod and staff of authority for the comfort, protection and well being of their 'lambs.'

The sadness of any society across the centuries can be gauged by children being robbed of their parent's 'shepherd heart.' Whatever the cause, the result of this loss turns parents or guardians into mere 'hirelings.' Such an attitude is spoken of by Jesus in John 10:12,13 as he who abandons the lambs because he cares nothing for them.

In commissioning Peter, Jesus gives advice which also holds true for parents. In John 21:15-17 Peter is called to be a shepherd over God's 'flock.' In Nestle's Greek text Peter is called to 'feed my lambs', 'shepherd the little sheep', and 'feed the little sheep.' Parents will easily identify with the need to feed their 'lambs' yet somehow or other may miss the implication of 'shepherding.'

The Lord has invested in parents the equivalent of the shepherd's rod. They have authority over their children. Unfortunately, what is too often missing is the shepherd's heart. Without it, the rod becomes a source of abuse rather than an expression of love and concern. Read the following

Proverbs and be aware of how differently they would be understood and applied by a shepherd's heart and that of a hireling.

'He who spares the rod hates his son, but he who loves him is careful to discipline him.' 13:24.

'Folly is bound up in the heart of a child, but the rod of discipline will drive it far from him.' 22:15

'Discipline your son, and he will give you peace he will bring delight to your soul.' 29:17.

The hireling will understand 'the rod' as a literal cane in all cases and wield it without mercy or justice. However the 'rod of discipline' has wider meaning. It can be a metaphor as in the case of 'the rod of his mouth.' Here is authority expressed in words. The rod may be withholding privileges, imposing duties, inflicting fines. The parent's shepherd heart, understanding his/her 'lamb' knows the best use of the most appropriate 'rod.'

One day we parents will be called to account for the use of the rod of authority entrusted to us. On that day may our children stand with us and speak on our behalf such words as are written in the Shepherd Psalm: 'your rod and your staff, they comforted me.' (verse 4b.)

Prayer: Good Shepherd anoint my head with your oil, lead me by your still waters, help me understand your use of your rod and staff so I might be an under-shepherd to those in my care. Amen.

Reflection/ Action: What does it mean to have a shepherd's heart? Am I comforting and protecting my 'flock?'

Day 26

The Beauty of the Unseen Child

Reading: Psalm 139

Key verse: *But now, this is what the Lord says – he who created you, O Jacob, he who formed you O Israel: 'Fear not, for I have redeemed you; I have summoned you by name; you are mine.'*

Isaiah 43:1

We live in a marvellous technological age with an almost overwhelming influx of knowledge. Previously unseen and unknown features within the body have been made known by such machines as the ultrasound. This has revealed the hidden world of the womb and the baby to astounded viewers. The Psalmist, by contrast, graphically presents 'still pictures' by his inspired insights of the unseen child.

Psalm 139:13 'You created my inmost being; you knit me together in my mother's womb.' David, the writer, portrays birth as an ongoing masterpiece of God's creative work. When the Lord God created Adam and Eve He instructed them to be fruitful and multiply. Within the security and joy of marriage children were to be conceived, born and nurtured. From Psalm 139 we gain the impression that God did not merely pre-program Adam and Eve for conception, then withdraw, rather, God is seen by David as taking both D.N.A. streams and knitting them together to form new life.

Psalm 139:14 'I praise you because I am fearfully and wonderfully made;' every birth verifies this statement. Each child is precious. Why? Because, the boy or girl carries the imprimatur, the finger print of God's Image within. This remains true regardless of any nasty complications which affect the baby's body or mind development. We live in a world that disregards the health and holiness principles of God with unfortunate consequences. Too often such consequences affect the conception and development of the unborn child.

It is the understanding of each individual's preciousness that gives us all a sense of personal worth, despite seen or unseen limitations. Every advance in our understanding of our body, mind, and emotions, keeps on affirming what the Scriptures said and keeps repeating, 'we are fearfully and wonderfully made!'

Psalm 139:15 'My frame was not hidden from you when I was made in the secret place. When I was woven together in the depths of the earth, your eyes saw my unformed body.' The womb as the secret place is likened to the depths of the earth and yet it is not hidden from God's eyes. He sees what is happening. He is interested. He is involved in so far as permitted. What the baby perhaps senses, in maturity he or she knows by faith the truth of verses 11 and 12, 'If I say, "surely the darkness will hide me and the light become night around me," even the darkness will not be dark to you; the night will shine like the day, for darkness is as light to you.'

There is a beautiful thought wrapped up in the word 'woven.' It means to embroider. God embroiders the body and personality of the baby with His creative skill. He takes what is available and weaves something beautiful. It's as though He is one of the tapestry weavers of Exodus 28:39 intent on making beautiful curtains and garments for worship and service in the Tabernacle. The Psalmist envisages the Lord's weaving ability, talent and creative forces being invested into the child that one day will be used to worship and serve Him.

Psalm 139:17 sums up the impact upon our consciousness when we remember our Creator and Redeemer, 'How precious to me are your thoughts O God! How vast is the sum of them.'

Prayer: There are times Heavenly Father when I find it difficult to respond to some young or older people because of their appearance or manner. Bring me to my knees so I can draw from your love and acceptance to love and accept such people. You accepted me, unworthy as I am, help me deliberately and graciously reach out and accept others in your Name. Amen.

Reflection/ Action: When I look at a child, especially a child with congenital disabilities, do I believe they are precious to God? How do I reflect that in my approach to them and their carers?

Day 27

The Promised Child

Reading: Genesis 3:1-21

Key verse: *For to us a child is born, to us a son is given, and the government will be upon his shoulders. And he will be called Wonderful Counsellor, Mighty God, Everlasting Father, Prince of Peace.* Isaiah 9:6

There is a ring of expectation throughout the Judeo-Christian Scriptures. Someone is coming fills its pages. The first thirty-nine books vibrate with hope and anticipation of the promised one. Who was it the nation longed for, to whom the prophets pointed? It was to a child.

From Genesis 3:15 comes the first revelation of this promised child. It is uttered by the Lord God as He dealt with Adam and Eve's betrayal and treason. To the Serpent (Satan) who instigated this rebellion God said, 'I will put enmity between you and the woman, and between your offspring (seed) and hers (seed).' Paul tells us in Galatians 3:16 that this pointed to Christ Jesus.

In Isaiah 7:14 we have a further development of this promise, 'Therefore the Lord Himself will give you a sign: The virgin will be with child and will give birth to a son and will call him Emmanuel' (God with us). This promise was unveiled in an historical incident in Isaiah's day which pointed beyond it to the account we read in Matthew and Luke. The promised one will be of the woman, he will be special and his name will reveal his origin, 'God with us.'

As you read Isaiah time and again you come across this child and what he will be and do. Unnamed, except for 'Emmanuel', the reader is presented with some fascinating insights as to his character and authority.

In Isaiah chapter 9:6,7, the Christmas passage, are claims for this child either extravagant and outrageous, or they are prophetic and true. What is written has the feel of Heaven. God is outlining His intentions and in so doing throws out a challenge to His enemies to prevent it. Their attempts, culminating in King Herod's Bethlehem baby onslaught, failed.

This promised child was destined to carry the government of the world 'on his shoulders.' We are living in an age in which the nations are increasingly perplexed and anxious in the face of ever mounting terror, economic uncertainty, racial and religious tensions, inequalities and injustices. God has spoken of a day coming when His child, born of a virgin will step in with righteousness and justice, with power and authority. He will reign. The nations will yield.

Isaiah goes further in his testimony to this promised child. In chapter 11:1-5 we are given insights into the child's historical lineage as well as his character and spirit. This child will be related to the kingly line being 'a shoot…from the stump of Jesse…' From the tribe of Judah and King David in His lineage. Once again we have a 'loud whisper' as to the attempts to eradicate the human genealogy of the promised child. The 'stump' seemed finished until the unfailing promise and providence of God brought forth the 'shoot.'

The rebellion and self will of Adam turned an earthly paradise into the realm of death and corruption. Yahweh did not walk away from the challenge thrown down by Satan's delusion. The Lord said, 'Someone is coming.' He will come as the seed of the woman, and he will make possible reconciliation between Creator and the created. Heaven one day would say that Someone has come so 'Behold the Child!'

Prayer: Let the Heavens ring out the news, the Promised One has come. Lord, let your people repeat the glorious refrain, Emmanuel has come! Praise be to your name for the faithfulness of your promises concerning the One we know as Jesus.

Reflection/ Action: Am I looking forward to the Lord's return? 1 John 2:28.

Day 28

The Child Who Came

Reading: Luke 2:1-39

Key verse: *Christ Jesus: Who being in very nature God... made himself nothing, taking the very nature of a servant, being made in human likeness.* Philippians 2:6,7

How would you recognise the promised baby when he arrived? Across the centuries men and some women have pushed themselves forward as 'the promised one.' Their names have been swallowed up in the dust of history, their followers doomed to an eternal regret. In John 5:39 Jesus issued an invitation to people of His day, and every day since; 'You diligently study the Scriptures because you think that by them you possess eternal life. These are the Scriptures that testify about me.'

Jesus is saying, 'Check me out! See if I fill out the shadow thrown up by the 39 books.' The Gospels are a record of four authors who did just that. Matthew, Mark, Luke and John show us various aspects of Jesus, fleshing out the shadow for their respective readers. The Gospels resonate with the theme, 'Someone has come.' Luke and Matthew in particular begin with the promised child and his affect on those who came to meet him.

In Luke 2:1-39 we come across three incidents surrounding the birth of the One named Jesus. Luke is a very thorough historian. What he has written has been the result of research and interview, overseen by the Holy Spirit.

To an unrecorded number of shepherds Heaven's angels declared the arrival of the promised Child. Humanly speaking, God seems to present His child's credentials and purposes to the most unlikely, the most neglected, the most powerless of people. Shepherds were despised, considered untrustworthy and denied the right to be a witness in court. Luke informs us that Heaven came to these men with the news the nation has been waiting for. 'Today in the town of David a saviour has been born to you; he is Christ the Lord.' Doesn't that tell us something of the Lord's heart for the poor and downtrodden! The shepherds didn't keep it a secret either as they returned to their flock. It makes you wonder if any of those so informed followed up their story.

Forty one days after Mary had given birth to Jesus she makes her way to the temple. She presents the prescribed sacrifice of purification and consecrates her first born to the Lord God. As Mary proceeds to do this an aged devout and righteous man named Simeon intercepts her. Taking Jesus in his arms Simeon praised God for this child who would be the achiever of salvation, the light of revelation to the Gentiles, the glory of Israel. Simeon was convinced that the promised child was the Child who had come.

Mary and Joseph must have been totally overwhelmed by this experience. It was capped off by an old lady named Anna. She was a prophetess who spent her days in the temple. Seeing the baby, Anna gave thanks to God. She also spoke about the child to all who were looking forward to the redemption of Jerusalem.

Why is it some are more receptive than others to follow up the news about the fulfilment of the promised One? Maybe unbelief or the cares of daily life had smothered the expectation. Their failure to check it out robbed them of many blessings.

Someone is coming, has turned into, Someone has come. Before our eyes and ears are the testimonies of those who participated in the drama. The Lord God of Glory invites you to check out the One Isaiah called Emmanuel, the Angels called the Christ and Mary under instructions called Him, Jesus. Don't allow other things impede your search and deny you the joy of knowing Him who has come in the name of the Lord.

Prayer: Arouse me eternal God with a sense of anticipation in gaining a deeper understanding of the Christmas event so I may appreciate Jesus in a more meaningful way. Amen.

Reflection/ Action: I will search the Scriptures with a 'hungry heart' to know more about the One I call my Lord and my God, even Jesus!

Day 29

The Child of Nazareth

Reading: Luke 2:39-52.

Key verse: *And a voice from heaven said, 'This is my Son, whom I love; with him I am well pleased.'* Matthew 3:17

I wonder what it would have been like to be a parent to Jesus? If he was my elder brother, how would we have played, learnt, laughed and cried together? The Gospels don't provide any answers. Luke does give us a brief glimpse of the upbringing Jesus enjoyed as a Jewish boy in a spiritually devout home.

The home is meant to be the fashioning, educating, equipping centre for a child to grow and flourish as an adult. The Scriptures uphold the parents' privilege and responsibility in the moral, spiritual and educational teaching of their child or children.

'The child grew and became strong; he was filled with wisdom, and the grace of God was upon him.' (Luke 2:40) Growing up under Roman occupation and in unsettled times would not have been easy. As a child in a devout Jewish family Jesus would have been confronted by people and practices hostile to God's covenant and promises. What he learnt at home and in the synagogue and saw in the temple equipped him with wisdom in mixing with and talking with all manner of people. His was no secluded upbringing, isolated from life's harsh realities. However, in his home life and with his parents' faith and example Jesus knew security and joy. Surely this is the right of every child.

As a growing boy Jesus developed his physical and mental prowess. He was no mindless hulk or insipid nerd. His strength and mental ability set in motion in childhood can be discerned in what he did and endured in manhood. Jesus is an example of a fully developed personality well worth aspiring to in one's own life.

'The fear of the Lord is the beginning of wisdom; all who follow his precepts have good understanding.' (Psalm 111:10) Such holy reverence for the word of God, His worship and Covenant would have been the atmosphere of Jesus' home life. This is more than an intellectual appreciation. Wisdom comes from applying theory into everyday situations. Faith grows by obeying God's word despite opposition and difficulties. Jesus joined both together in his heart and actions.

I have to admit, I would like to know the outworking of the grace of God in Jesus' life as a child. Perhaps it is that unmerited favour the Lord God wishes to share with every child and adult, but is prohibited by ignorance or disobedience. What Jesus enjoyed and experienced is still available for us today. The apostle Peter urges his readers to 'Grow in the grace and knowledge of our Lord and Saviour Jesus Christ. To Him be glory both now and forever. Amen.' (2 Peter 3:18)

'Jesus grew in wisdom and stature, and in favour with God and men.' He was under the scrutiny of his village and what they saw, they appreciated. He had to prove himself as a son, a student, and as a tradesman with his carpenter 'father' Joseph. Proverbs 3:3, 4 may have been in Luke's mind as he penned the words above. 'Let love and faithfulness never leave you; bind them around your neck, write them on the tablet of your heart. Then you will win favour and a good name in the sight of God and man.'

The child of Nazareth did that. He did find favour although they found it hard to come to grips with His ministry. Jesus did express sadness when he said, 'a prophet is not without honour, except in his own city.' However, Jesus is without doubt that village's most illustrious son.

Prayer: May my home be a place where Jesus feels 'at home' and where family and visitors sense His presence. Thank you Lord for sharing our humble surrounding with us. Amen.

Reflection/ Action: What impresses me about the family life of Jesus?

Day 30

When it will be Safe to Play

Reading: Isaiah 11:1-9

Key verse: *O Lord, you are my God; I will exalt you and praise your name, for in perfect faithfulness you have done marvellous things, things planned long ago.*   Isaiah 25:1

Tears are the diet of parents. Danger is the playmate of children. Is there a day when tears will cease, danger be forgotten? Isaiah 11:6-9 points to just such a time. 'The wolf will live with the lamb, the leopard will lie down with the goat, the calf and the lion and the yearling together; and a little child will lead them....The infant will play near the hole of the cobra, and the young child put his hand into the viper's nest.'

This will come about because the Someone promised and the Someone who came is the Someone who will come again. The Christian faith declares that this Someone is Jesus. 'This same Jesus, who has been taken from you into heaven, will come back in the same way you have seen him go into heaven.' Acts 1:11. The disciples saw Jesus literally, physically ascend. When He returns it will be visible and physical onto the Mount of Olives. The prophet Zechariah looked forward to that day and said so in Zechariah 14:3.

From the tumult will arise a new and glorious period in which the promises of God spelt out in numerous passages of the Old Testament will be activated. This will be when Jesus rules from Jerusalem, as promised by the angel announcing the Lord God's choice for Mary to be the mother of the Messiah. Luke 1:31-33. 'You will...give birth to a son, and you are to...name him Jesus. He will be great and will be called the Son of the Most high. The Lord God will give him the throne of his father David and he will reign over the house of Jacob forever; his kingdom will never end.' The prophet Isaiah in chapter 2:1-5, declares righteousness and justice will then be the order of the day. The cry of individuals and nations for 'Peace!' will at last be enjoyed. The curse that Adam's sin and rebellion caused to fall on this planet will be removed. What is inferred in the original picture of the Garden of Eden will be a wonderful, tangible reality.

The prophets draw our attention to this time in many ways. The ones I like are associated with God's tender interest in children, the lame and the frail. 'See, I will bring from the land of the north and gather them from the ends of the earth. Among them will be the blind and the lame, expectant mothers and women in labour; a great throng will return… Then maidens will dance and be glad, young men and old as well. I will turn their mourning into gladness…' Jeremiah 31:8, 13.

'This is what the Lord Almighty says: "Once again men and women of ripe old age will sit in the streets of Jerusalem…The city streets will be filled with boys and girls playing there."' Zechariah 8:4, 5.

We know that this will happen. On what do we base this hope and assurance? It springs from the faithfulness of God to His word. We can bank our lives on it because of Jesus. He came the first time as promised. We can check out Jesus in the Gospels as the Someone who has come. Because of the cross and resurrection Jesus has triumphed over the forces of wickedness and Death. The promise still stands He will return. As we keep Jesus as the focus of our life, the future, in spite of present difficulties, is worth waiting for.

Imagine being a child and playing with a lion, wow! No fear. No danger, therefore no tears. Imagine being a parent and watching your child put a hand into a snakes nest. Ooooh!

As Isaiah saw it, 'The Sovereign Lord will wipe away the tears from all faces; He will remove the disgrace of His people from all the earth. The Lord has spoken. (Isaiah 25:8) It will be a great time to be a child.

Prayer: Come Jesus! Come, this world is in dire need of your rule!

Reflection/ Action: I will live in anticipation of this coming event and look forward to the time I will see Jesus as Lord, face to face.

Day 31

Becoming Children of God

Reading: John 1:1-18

Key verse: *How great is the love the Father has lavished on us, that we should be called children of God! And that is what we are!*
1 John 3:1

In recent times men have asked the courts to decide maternity and paternity suits using D.N.A technology. This has arisen over doubts about who is the real father of the child. The relationship of the child especially to the man will hinge on whether or not the boy or girl has matching D.N.A.

Within the spiritual realm all types of people make claims about being children of God. Now the Lord is the Creator according to the Scriptures. That is not the basis on which to make a claim to being related to God. An assessment as to your personal status cannot be made by religious affinity, moral behaviour or a ceaseless round of being nice and doing good. When you and I stand before the Lord God on Judgement day all such status claims will evaporate before His gaze. When we stand before Him He will be looking for evidence of His D.N.A flowing in our spirit. 'If anyone does not have the Spirit of Christ, he does not belong to Christ.' (Romans 8:9)

How is this spiritual D.N.A. defined?

'When Christ, who is your life appears then you also will appear with Him in glory.' (Colossians 3:4) God the Father will be looking for the tell tale signs of a personal encounter with Jesus as the Christ, your personal Saviour and Lord. The apostle Paul stresses the need for such an experience in these words, 'My dear children, for whom I am again in the pains of childbirth *until Christ be formed in you.*' (Galatians 4:19, emphasis added)

How is it possible for Christ to be formed within a man or woman?

'To all who received Him (Jesus) to those who believed in His name, He gave the right to become children of God – children born not of natural descent, nor of human decision or a husband's will, but born of God.' (John 1:12,13)

Notice the requirement!

Receiving Jesus is preceded by knowing certain things about Him and being convinced of their truth to the point of bowing the will in obedient surrender. Those things required to know about Jesus are summed up in John 20:31 'These are written that you may believe that Jesus is the Christ (the promised Messiah) the Son of God (His unique birth into this world and relationship with God the Father) and that by believing you may have life in His name.'

You may ask, 'What has been written?'

The answer is in the Gospels, especially the gospel of John. There you see the credentials of Jesus and what He experienced on the cross, and why. None of this would be of interest to anyone except for the resurrection of Jesus from the tomb. This fact of history places Jesus on the World stage as conqueror of Death and Sin and therefore Saviour and Lord. This in turn confronts all of us with a choice, to follow Him or reject Him? 'Christ's love compels us, because we are convinced that one died for all, and therefore all died. And He died for all, that those who live should no longer live for themselves but for Him who died for them and was raised again.' (2 Corinthians 5:14, 15)

When you believe the Truth and make a personal choice to accept Jesus as Lord and Saviour God implants His D.N.A. in your spirit. This is called being born again. This gives you the right to call Him, 'Our Father.' This gives you the assurance of being accepted by God into His presence for all eternity. 'You did not receive a spirit that makes you a slave to fear, but you received the Spirit of sonship. And by him we cry 'Abba, Father.' The Spirit Himself testifies with our spirit that we are God's children. Now if we are children, then we are heirs – heirs of God and co-heirs with Christ…' (Romans 8:15-17)

Being children of God has its responsibilities as well as privileges. You will become aware of them as you read God's Word and worship Him in the fellowship of His Church.

Prayer: Heavenly Father, I adore you for all you have done in my life. I praise you for my Lord and Saviour Jesus and His awesome victory on the cross. To you Holy Spirit I give thanks for your bringing me to know the Gospel and to believe it. Almighty God, Father, Son and Holy Spirit, make me your faithful child for your glory in time and eternity. Amen.

Reflection/ Action: Have I yielded my life to Jesus and allowed Him to dwell in me? If so, do I rejoice in the Biblical picture of being 'God's temple?' If I have never yielded my life to Jesus as Lord and Saviour I will do so now and by faith know His acceptance.

I See A Child.

I see a child in war torn lands
Hungry, frightened, bleeding hands
Outstretched, begging, seeking comfort
From a world where he is caught
In turmoil beyond his understanding
And all he can do is dream.

I see a child in a shanty town
Abused, confused, eyes cast down
Hope still born, dignity robbed
Childhood's innocence defiled
By predators young and old
And all she can do is dream.

I see a child, someone's shame
Neglected for fortune and fame
Living in a mansion high
Knowing a dark ghetto inside
Tortured by quiet, ceaseless screams
And all he can do is dream.

Do you see those children too?
Have you seen their broken hearts
Carved within bodies of fear
Unwashed faces stained by tears
Trembling lips play their theme
And all they can do is dream.

Come, it's passed time to begin
To hear the children sing,
A new day where dreams come true
When such people as me and you
Seek to change their daily scene
And give them more than dreams.

Ray Hawkins